Explorabook®

A Kids' Science Museum
in a Book

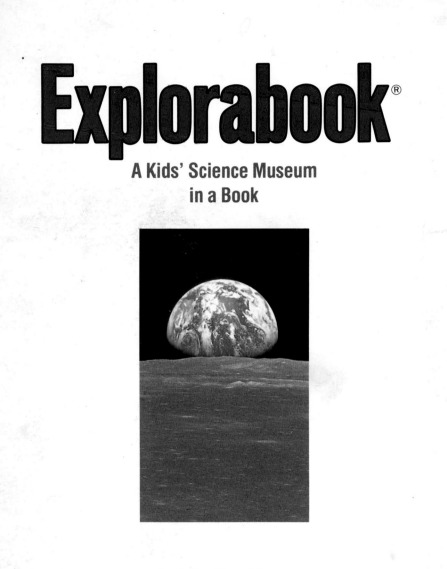

John Cassidy
The Exploratorium

Klutz Press • Palo Alto, CA

MR. BACTERIA

Illustrations:
Elwood Smith (cartoons)
Ed Taber (instructive art)

Photo research:
John Cassidy, MaryEllen Podgorski,
Stuart Kenter, Lindsay Kefauver.
All credits appear on last page.

Book Design:
MaryEllen Podgorski

Graphic Production:
Elizabeth Buchanan, Suzanne Gooding

Sourcing and Manufacturing:
DeWitt Durham

Book is manufactured in Korea;
Fresnel lens and diffraction grating,
Taiwan; Agar, moiré spinner, mirror,
U.S.A. The moiré spinner was designed
for us by Tony Jenkinson. Additional
spinners are available through our
mail order catalogue. See inside back
cover for details.

ISBN 1-878257-14-5

4 1 5 8 5 7

Acknowledgments

The Explorabook was a major project
that was years in development. During
that time a great many people contrib-
uted to the effort. The amount of time
and help, unfortunately, foredoom the
following list to incompleteness. Our
apologies to all those whose names we
left out.

Amongst the Exploratorium staff: Dave
Barker, Charles Carlson, Ron Hipschman,
Barry Kluger-Bell, Claire Pillsbury,
Nic Sammond, and Rob Semper stormed
their brains in our development meet-
ings and did final readings. Deborah O.
Raphael was enormously helpful in the
area of home-grown bacterial infesta-
tions. Kurt Feichtmeir was midwife to
the project in its earliest stages and
active cheerleader in its later.

Other readers and contributors included
Gary Mcdonald, Heather Cassidy, Sidney
Raffle, Martin Gardner, Jeff Busby, Scott
Stillinger, and Nancy Cassidy.

Ebony Haight, Beckett Haight, Camilla
Reynolds, Jesse Herzog and Gary
Mcdonald (bless them all) were our
photographers' models, and Antique
Interiors West, Palo Alto, helped
with props.

Overlording the Exploratorium's effort,
and co-conspirator from the very beginning, was Pat Murphy, one-third of our
Irish Triumvirate.

Finally, an enormous share of credit
goes to Paul Doherty of the Exploratorium. Nearly all the facts in this book
are a result of his expertise and tireless
enthusiasm. All of the errors, meanwhile, are part of my contribution.

   John Cassidy,
   Palo Alto, Spring 1991

Contents

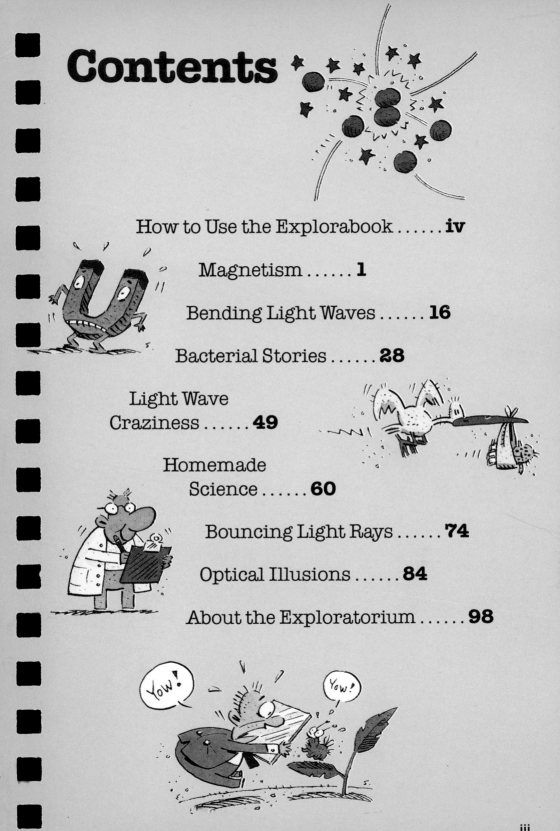

How to Use the Explorabook

First of all, please do not simply read this book. If you own the Explorabook for more than a few hours, and do not bend or smear any of its pages, nor tear open the agar packets, nor attempt to lose the attached magnet, then you are probably not using it correctly. It is a tool. Please treat it that way.

The book is divided into seven sections. You'll see the subject headings in the table of contents. Except for the section titled Homemade Science, each section contains the special tools you'll need to do the described activities.

The Explorabook is written for people who tend to sit toward the back during scientific lectures. It assumes that you remember nothing of what happened in your science classes, assuming you ever took any. In fact, the only thing you need to bring to this book and its activities is a willingness to ask irritating and difficult questions of the people and the world around you.

Fortunately, that kind of curiosity is basic to human nature. You were born with it. Don't fight it, and don't let anyone else discourage it. Einstein once described himself as being not terribly intelligent, just extremely inquisitive. It was in that playful and pestering spirit that the Explorabook was conceived—a celebration of that most human and hopeful trait, curiosity.

Magnetism

Magnetism

What Is It?

It's a magnet—absolutely one of Mother Nature's funnest playthings. The name "magnet," incidentally, comes from "Magnesia," an area near ancient Greece where natural magnets were commonly found.

How Can I Play With It?

There are many, many ways. But let's start with a mental exercise. Pretend you're from another universe and have never seen a magnet before. Never in your entire life. Try to clear your mind <u>completely</u> of all magnetic memories.

Then, with your empty mind, just explore. Put your magnet onto something steel (a refrigerator is the classic example). What happens? THE MAGNET JUST STICKS THERE! Think

about that for a moment. Ask yourself: Is this normal? How can this possibly be happening? What would the ancient Greeks have made of this? (Even better, pretend you're an ancient Greek and propose a theory that explains what you're seeing.)

Experiment Number "Excuse Me, Sir, But Which Way to the North Pole?"

When you have two magnets, it doesn't take long to discover that sometimes they repel each other, and sometimes they attract. It depends on which "poles" are facing each other. Any magnet has two poles, North and South. Opposite poles attract (North pulls on South) and similar poles repel (North pushes away North). If you had two magnets, you could demonstrate this very easily.

Fortunately, you <u>do</u> have two magnets. The 2-inch-long magnet in your hand, and the 8,000-mile-wide one you're standing on. Here's a way to discover where the poles of your bigger magnet (the planet Earth) are.

Magnet #1

Magnet #2

Take a piece of thread; tie one end to the magnet, and tape the other end to the edge of a table. Let the magnet hang for a few minutes in mid-air until it stops twisting. Whichever side of the magnet is facing you, mark that side with a piece of tape. If you were to set off walking in that direction, you would eventually come to one or the other of the Earth's magnetic poles.

Experiment Number 2
Construct an Anti-Gravity Machine

This is not as difficult as you've been led to believe. You'll need a drinking glass, your magnet, a bit of tape, and a foot or so of thread. Set the magnet on the glass as illustrated. Tie the thread to the clip and stick it to the magnet. Tape the thread to the table and begin pulling the thread gradually through the tape until you've pulled the clip off the magnet. Keep pulling until the clip is an inch or so from the magnet. Stick the tape down extra-hard to keep the thread from pulling through anymore.

Leave the clip there, suspended in mid-air, straining on its leash, caught in a real-live "tractor beam." Pretty amazing.

As you watch the clip pulling on the thread, focus on the empty space between the clip and the magnet. There's a force at work here somewhere. The first question that probably occurs to you is: "Can I block it?"

Time for some low-cost experiments. Put a piece of fabric in the space; don't touch either the magnet or the clip. Anything happen? How about a piece of plastic? Aluminum? Glass? A penny? Paper? Stick your whole finger in there. What happens?

Now try another paper clip, or a fork. What happens now?

So now the question is: "Why do some things cause the clip to drop, and others don't?" For the answer, you'll have to keep reading, and keep experimenting.

Magnets Making Magnets

Stick a paper clip to your magnet. Then put another paper clip to the first one. It sticks. The magnetism seems to run through the first clip. Then put a third clip on the second. It sticks. Amazing. But now try this. Carefully pull the first clip off the magnet and see what happens. The three-clip chain stays together! The clips have been turned into little magnets on their own. They've been converted!

To deconvert your new little magnets, all you need to do is vibrate their atoms. How do you vibrate their atoms? Simple. Drop them off a table. When the paper clip atoms hit the ground, they vibrate. Result? Slightly less organized atoms and plain old non-magnetic paper clips.

Our own verified record for a paper clip chain from the magnet provided with this book is seven. We have one unconfirmed report of eight right here in our midst, but the person involved has been unable to reproduce his results with anyone else in the room, a circumstance that we find suspicious.

To give you another chance to see this phenomenon of magnets making magnets (known as "induced magnetism") in action, let me include a high-quality little magic trick that depends on it. I call it...

Dinnertime Magic

First off, you should know that good magic depends on good lying. So if you have any honesty hang-ups, put them aside. This is show-time.

Take your magnet and strap it with a belt or shoelace or something to the top of your thigh underneath your skirt or pants. Once that's done, all you need is a trusting dinner table audience, a fork, and a paper clip. Here's how it goes.

You're at the dinner table (wooden, not metal), surrounded by innocent family and friends. Cross your legs so that your magnet is pressed tight against the underside of the table. Your paper clip is in your shirt pocket. During a lull in the conversation, mention something interesting. Mention that you've been able to bond certain metals, one to the other, with a mentally powered cold fusion process. It's a very lightweight bond, of course, and also temporary since it only works during moments of intense concentration, but all in all, a pretty impressive personal achievement.

Perhaps your audience would like to see a demonstration?

Push the paper clip <u>directly</u> over the hidden magnet and gently place the fork on top of it. Close your eyes. Moan. Take a noisy deep breath, hold it, and puff out your cheeks.

Then open your eyes, drop your magnetized leg away from the table, and very carefully lift the fork up. The clip will stick to it. Stand up and gently wave the fork and clip around for effect.

After a few seconds of demonstration (during which your face should be turning red), exhale in a burst and simultaneously give the fork an <u>invisible</u> shake. The clip will drop loose. Bang the fork once against the table-top (this is important) and then pass both the fork and clip around for inspection. Don't worry, it won't work for anyone else.

How did you do that? By placing the fork and clip over the magnet, you were able to "convert" them into magnets (weak magnets, but still…). By rapping the fork on the table, you demagnetized it for everyone else.

..AND THAT MEANS YOU!

And remember, a good magician <u>never</u> reveals the secret.

What's Going On Here?

If you were to cut your magnet in half, you would have two smaller magnets, each with a N and S pole. Then, if you were to cut both of those pieces, you would find you had four magnets. Four more cuts, and you'd own eight small magnets. In fact, it turns out, if you continued cutting and cutting smaller pieces until finally you were down to a single atom, you would discover that the atom behaved like a magnet, with a N and S pole.

Now, you might try the same experiment with a regular piece of iron—non-magnetic. You could cut it in half and have two pieces of non-magnetized iron. Cut again, four pieces of non-magnetized iron. On and on you could cut, smaller and smaller pieces, none of them magnetized. Finally you'd come to the last stop, the atom. You'd test it, expecting the same result as always. But, amazingly, you'd find the iron atom <u>does</u> behave like a magnet. What gives?

The iron atom's magnetism comes from a component particle of the atom, a spinning particle called the electron. Normally electrons are paired together with opposite spins. The net result is no magnetic field. But with iron, some of the electrons are unpaired. The spins of these unpaired electrons tend to line up together, and when they do, they form tiny "pockets" of magnetism called "magnetic domains."

In a piece of regular, non-magnetized iron, these pockets are disorganized. They point one way or the other. The net effect is no magnet. But in a piece of magnetized iron, the pockets of magnetism <u>are</u> organized. They all pull in the same direction. Net effect? A magnet.

A non-magnetized nail

Because of the structure of its atoms, iron is a particularly good material to make magnets out of, but nickel, cobalt, and some man-made alloys also work. The vast majority of things, of course, don't work so well.

A magnetized nail

Any piece of iron (a nail or paper clip, for example) is a magnet waiting to be made. All it needs is to get its "pockets" of permanent magnetism organized. You could turn an ordinary nail into a magnet just by putting it beside your wand (a permanent magnet) and tapping it hard enough to organize its "domains."

Temporary Magnets

Not all magnets are permanent, of course. In fact, temporary magnets are millions of times more common, and millions of times more useful. But what's a "temporary magnet"? And how is one made?

By getting electrons to move. When electrons move in a stream (which they do all the time—we call it an electric current) they do an amazing thing. They automatically create a magnetic field around themselves. A good thing, too, because if they didn't, there would be no such thing as TV. There would be no such thing as hair dryers. No cyclotrons, no popcorn poppers, no stereos, no anything that used motors, sensors, video displays, or a zillion other "electromagnetic devices." The truth is, if tomorrow, all of a sudden, moving electrons stopped creating magnetic fields around themselves, the modern world as we know it would just about come to a halt.

41

Although we can only guess the name of the woman who invented the wheel, the name of the person who made this equally important discovery (the relationship between electrons in transit and magnetism) is well known, and the exact moment is even pinpointed. His name was Hans Christian Oersted and the year was 1819.

Hans Christian Oersted

Oersted was a professor at the University of Copenhagen and he was demonstrating to his students the fact that electricity, as it passed through a wire, would cause it to grow warm. ("The toaster effect").

A coil of wire on his bench was connected to a battery through a switch. The students were gathered around for the demonstration. An assistant threw the switch and the world changed forever. Because next to the coil (probably by accident) was a magnetic compass. When the switch was thrown, the needle suddenly veered from the north and pointed toward the wire. Oersted noticed this and promptly forgot about heating wires. He told the assistant to throw the switch off. The needle went back to north. The electrons moving through the wire had created a temporary magnet, an electromagnet. In a single instant, Oersted had discovered the fundamental bond between moving electrons and magnetism. Modern technology was off and running.

Experiment Number 4
Re-Inventing the
Electromagnetic Wheel

Oersted's epoch-making discovery is an easy one to duplicate. Get a flashlight battery and piece of wire (length doesn't matter). Strip the insulation off the ends of the wire and tape one of them to one end of the flashlight battery.

Now you need to make a magnetic compass. You'll need two styrofoam cups, the magnet that came with this book, and a needle. Cut a disk of styrofoam about the size of a nickel out of one of the cups. Fill the other cup half-full with water and float your styrofoam disk in it. Put one end of the needle on the magnet for a second, then lay it on the floating styrofoam. Don't let the needle touch the water.

Now you're in exactly the same position Hans Oersted was in 1819. After the needle stabilizes and points in one direction (it is, incidentally, the north-south direction) lay the wire across the top of the cup, parallel to the needle. With a drumroll, touch the bare end of the wire to the other end of the battery. What happens?

Touching the wire to the battery is your "switch." By turning it on and off in time, you might be able to get the needle compass to start turning around and around in circles. It doesn't take much imagination to see that there's a machine in here waiting to be built. With a slightly larger wire, and a slightly larger needle (plus a few gears, wheels, little tiny horses, and so forth) it might be possible to build a floating merry-go-round for fleas out of this contraption.

Actually, it's completely possible. In fact, flea merry-go-rounds are just the start of it. The principle you are looking at when you watch that needle swing around as you time your on-and-off power pulses is precisely what drives every electric motor ever built, up to and including the one driving the JetStream Hair Dryer and Brain Transfer Helmet pictured here.

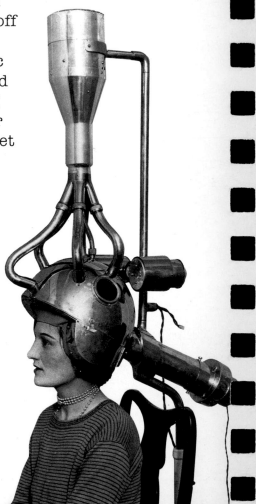

Activity:
Jumping Wires and the Northern Lights

Just as you did for your cup compass, tape the ends of a wire to a battery and lay the middle of the wire across the top of a cup. Now push your magnet wand into the cup, past the wire without touching it. The closer you can get to the wire, the more you will see it jump.

The reason, as you and Hans Oersted know, is that magnets push on moving electrons.

If your little magnet wand could get a wire to jump, imagine what the Earth-magnet could do if you could somehow get the entire planet next to a flowing electric charge.

Fortunately, that's already been arranged. Our Earth is almost always traveling through an electric current. The Sun throws bazillions of charged particles into outer space every second (the solar wind) and the planet is bathed in them. For the same reason that your wire jumped up, they are pushed toward one or the other of the magnetic poles, where they stream into the atmosphere with enough force to tear apart air atoms and molecules (exactly like lightning). When the particles recombine, they create the aurora, a fabulous natural light show that polar bears, Canadians, Antarctic penguin researchers, and many others, have been gazing at, and wondering about, for thousands of years.

The Knights of Knavery originally appeared in 1944 (Batman #25). Our version is reduced by about 85%, but we think it still retains all of its original punch. Reprinted by permission. Copyright © 1944, 1971 DC Comics Inc.

Bending Light Waves

Above: Two healthy hairs growing out of a clean human scalp. Dead and living skin cells surround them.

Far left: Another pair of hairs just emerging from the scalp.

Left: Two more strands chopped clean.

Bending Light Waves

What Is It?

In three words or less? A light bender. It's a Fresnel lens (pronounced "fray-nel'"). A sheet of plastic that has been manufactured with very precise bumps cut into it. The result? A magnifying lens of about four power. Four power simply means that things seen through this lens appear to be about four times normal size.

How Can I Play With It?

Go out and find some little tiny things to look at. For starters, I'd suggest bugs; they're close at hand, they're always willing and, when you see them up close, you'll be amazed all over again at how ugly they are.

As you marvel at your bug specimens, try to be fair and imagine what the experience is like from their point of view. Since the lens works both ways, both for you and the bug, you will be nothing but a monster eye in the sky to your specimen. Pretty frightening.

You can get a good idea of this bug's eye view of yourself with a game I call Weird Faces. It's an indoor game.

Activity:
Weird Faces

You'll need a partner. Give them the book and ask them to hold the lens in front of their face, as close as possible, while you stand about 10 steps back. Now give them the following instructions: "Look at me. Keep my face in the middle of the lens and move the lens away from your eyes—slowly—until you come to the end of your arms."

As you watch the lens, you'll see your partner's face slowly swell up, until the lens is entirely filled with a single bloodshot horror eye.

Activity: TV for Bats

Most bats spend their days hanging by their feet from cave ceilings. For them, it's very comfortable, but it obviously makes it impossible to watch TV.

Here's a solution to that problem. You'll need a television, a low table, a dark room, and a big sheet of white paper. A newspaper will work in a pinch. Set your book up on the low table, a few feet in front of the TV so that the Fresnel lens has a clear view of the screen.

Now hold your sheet of white paper behind the lens. Move the lens toward the book and away from it. Cover a few feet. You should see clear images of the TV at two different distances.

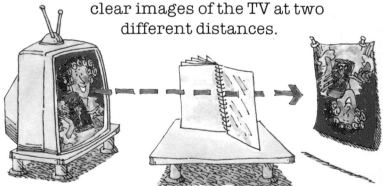

One of them will be small and bright, and one, large and dim. But both will be upside down.

As a final experiment, you can attach a chair to the ceiling, climb into it, hold on tight, and see what it's like to be a bat with a TV.

Activity: Nuclear-Cooked Hot Dog

Up to now, the activities have all been indoors. But what happens when you take your Fresnel lens out into the bright sunlight? In other words, what happens when you expose it to a ball of nuclear fusion 1,000,000 miles across?

The answer is—heat. A frightening amount. As a result, you have to be <u>extremely</u> careful, both with your eyes and your hands. A focused spot of sunlight can reach temperatures of **THOUSANDS** of degrees. It can burn you, or start a fire in a few seconds. As a result, there are two absolutely critical rules to follow with a Fresnel lens outdoors:

1. **Never stare directly at the pinpoint spot of concentrated light that a Fresnel lens creates.**

2. **Never focus that spot on anything flammable, or on any part of you.**

If you follow the above precautions, here's a quick and tasty activity. It's a recipe for "Roasted Hot Dog Slice." Not a big meal, but then it only takes a minute.

Cafe Le Hot
Cut a hot dog slice, fairly thin, take it outside and focus a spot on it about the size of the slice itself. In about a minute, it should begin to steam. Serve with a single potato chip. Yummy.

21

What's Going On Here?

Whenever you see something that's not glowing, it's because light has bounced off of it. Normally, light travels unbothered through clear space in straight lines. But sometimes, on its way to our eyes, it gets bent, bounced, split, twisted, or otherwise mangled by certain things—things like a drop of water, a pane of glass, a bottle of shampoo, or a Fresnel lens. Whenever this happens, the "thing" we're looking at, looks funny.

In the case of the Fresnel lens, since the bending is very organized, "funny"  means magnified, or enlarged. Straight sun light going into the lens is all "funneled" down to a point about 10 inches away from the lens's backside.

Light rays bend right at the surface between two things that are both clear or nearly clear. Light coming through the air is bent right at the surface of a swimming pool, but it is not bent once it gets into the pool.

Magnifying lenses work the same way. The light is bent right at their surface, right where the air and the glass meet. Inside the lens, there is no more bending.

A normal (glass) magnifying lens depends on a curved surface to do the right kind of organized bending. All the glass inside the lens is really unnecessary to the job.

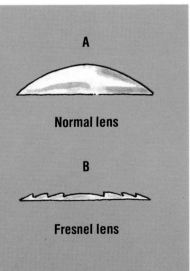

(A) A thick lens designed to converge, or focus, beams of light. All the real work is done at the top surface where the light is bent.

(B) Removing the interior of the lens (which doesn't really do anything anyway) leaves a flat, "all-surface" lens.

A

Normal lens

B

Fresnel lens

Serious Magnification

These photographs were taken through an instrument called a scanning electron microscope. While your Fresnel lens is a 4-power magnifier, a scanning electron microscope is potentially a 10-billion-power magnifier. Quite a difference.

In the case of the Fresnel lens, beams of light bounce off the Batman comic (for example), then are bent as they go through the Fresnel lens, and finally hit inside your eye.

In the case of the electron microscope, beams of electrons (much, much smaller "particles" than the photons of light) are bounced off the bug, bent in a magnetic field, then collected on a special wire. The image is seen displayed on a video screen.

The three photos at left, taken at increasing magnification, show mites burrowed into the back of a hedgehog flea. The mites use tiny suckers to live under the flea's scales. Poet Augustus de Morgan scribbled the following little verse which waited nearly 200 years for this perfect series of accompanying photos: "Great fleas have little fleas upon their backs to bite them, and little fleas have lesser fleas, and so ad infinitum."

A velvety tree ant looks around. She (he?) is actually about a quarter of an inch in size and is a native Californian. The photo was taken through a scanning electron microscope that magnifies by bending electron streams rather than light waves.

A tiny wasp emerges from the back of a pear psylla. The wasp has hatched from an egg and grown to maturity inside the larger insect. Lest you feel too sorry for the host insect, the psylla (which is about the size of this "0") is a major pest in the pear orchards of the Northwest.

Why a Rainbow?

Pure sunlight is composed of many different colors all mixed together into the white light that we all normally see. It is possible, however, to "un-mix" them all. If you pass a beam of sunlight through a drop of water, the beam is bent and bounced around inside the drop in a very specific way. When the beam leaves, each color has been bent a little differently. The result is an "un-mixed" beam of light. It's no longer white, it's a rainbow.

A beam of light going through a raindrop is bent going through the first surface, then it bounces off the back surface, and finally it leaves out the front surface again. Now it is much dimmer, and at an angle to its incoming line. Red leaves at 42 degrees, violet leaves at 40, and every other color at an angle in between. This spreading over 2 degrees is how the colors "un-mix."

Droplets of water are only shaped like teardrops when they are about to drop off of something (like a faucet). In mid-air, they are spheres.

Augustin Jean Fresnel,

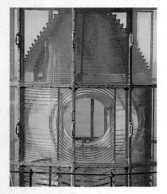

the 19th-century French scientist who invented this lens for use in lighthouses, realized that a lens big enough to focus a lighthouse beam would weigh tons— most of it useless interior glass. So he designed a lens that was "all surface," with no middle. It was one of those brilliantly simple ideas. Within 50 years, every operating lighthouse was equipped with one.

Incidentally, if you're thinking that this is the first Fresnel lens you've ever seen, you're off by a couple of million. Fresnel lenses are frequent components in that beloved modern convenience of ours— the traffic light. Perhaps you've been stuck at a red light at some point in your life. Ever wondered why the beam of red seem so personally directed at you? Why people on the sidewalk can't seem to see it directly?

There's a Fresnel lens placed in front of the bulb, bending the light for your eyes only.

Bacterial Stories

Sweat emerging from a pore in human skin, magnified by 500 times in a scanning electron microscope. The green spheres are bacteria and are the root cause of the problem the researchers pictured above are testing for. Bacteria, incidentally, are so plentiful on your skin that no amount of washing will ever get rid of all of them.

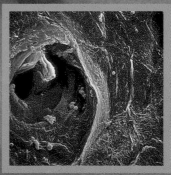

Bacterial Stories

MR. BACTERIA   MS. FUNGUS

What's In These Envelopes?

It's called "agar" (ah-gar), but you can think of it as bacteria snack food, or maybe fungi brunches. It comes from seaweed, and scientists have used it for years to grow bacteria and fungi on. There's enough here in these few packets to feed billions of hungry bacteria and fungi for weeks.

How Can I Play With It?

By inviting a large variety of fungal and bacterial guests into your home. Start by preparing their meals in your kitchen. This is easy cooking. The most important part is keeping everything very clean. With the two packets of agar here in the book, you can make two cups of agar gel, enough for three or four of the following experiments. (If you need more agar for additional research activities, there's an address in the back of the book.)

AGAR GEL

1. Get three clean, shallow glass bowls or saucers and one clean saucepan. Add contents of one envelope and one cup of water to saucepan. Get grown-up assistant. Ask assistant, nicely, to bring mixture to a boil, then turn off the heat. Then add one teaspoonful of sugar and stir until dissolved. Prepare to pour.

2. Assistant pours still-hot liquid into bowls, until it is ½ inch deep. Immediately cover with plastic wrap. Allow to cool, 30 minutes. Serves 6,000,000,000,000,000.

What you now have, hopefully, is hot, germ-free, nutrient-filled liquid, sitting in very clean containers, covered with a clean, air-tight plastic wrap. After the liquid cools, it should turn into a gel kind of stuff, delicious if you're a bacterium or fungus.

There. You're ready for your guests. But where are they? Actually, as you'll discover in a moment, the question should be, "Where aren't they?"

Take your mouth, for example. It's disgusting. A teeming, rich bacterial breeding ground. On your tongue alone there are probably several hundred different kinds of bacteria growing side-by-side. Meanwhile, in your insides, bacteria and fungi exist in uncountable millions, particularly in your lungs and intestines.

Around the house, additionally, you can find more bacteria almost everywhere. On your silverware, dishes, pots and pans, and towels. (Towels are especially full of them.)

Food, of course, is usually teeming with bacteria, as is juice, milk, etc. (Yogurt, beer, and cheese are actually <u>manufactured</u> with "domesticated" fungi or bacteria.)

Perhaps you doubt me. Herds of primitive life forms thriving on your just-cleaned fork? Fortunately, you don't have to trust me. If you've followed the steps above, you should have your "bacterial table" all set. Let's invite some guests, and you can see for yourself.

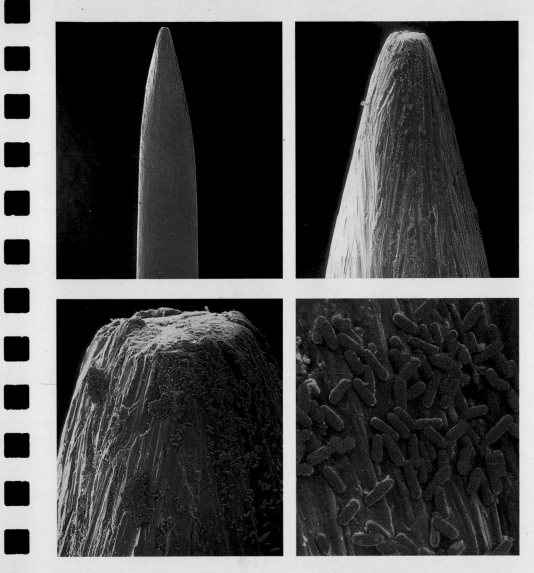

A series of photographs taken at increasing magnifications of the point of a household pin. The yellow rod-shapes are bacteria. The photographs were taken with a scanning electron microscope and then false-colored with the aid of a computer.

☞ **Beauty and the Bacteria**

A highly magnified view of the surface of a clean human tooth. The red worm-shapes are bacteria. Tooth decay, incidentally, is often caused by a waste product of bacterial digestion.

Experiment Number
Bacteria Safaris

LOOK FOR THESE HABITATS!

You can do this one with a shallow dish filled with a half-cup of agar gel.

1. Go find a roll of Scotch tape. Now prowl around the house looking for something where millions of bacteria or fungi might be hiding. Remember, this is not hard. The dog dish, a door knob, punch bowl, shaving brush, your silverware, the toilet seat, practically anything will do.

2. When you've chosen something, stick a piece of tape to it. Pull the tape up and stick it back down once or twice. Then take it and hurry back to your already prepared agar bowl.

3. Lift off the plastic wrap, press the sticky side of the tape down onto the gel surface, remove it, and immediately re-cover the gel.

4. Put your dish on a cool shelf somewhere out of the sun. Results will be about a week in coming.

NELLIE

Experiment Number
Bacteria Races

Another experiment for a shallow dish filled
with a half-cup of agar gel.

1. Take one of the agar dishes that you haven't
used yet and stick a long piece of tape on the bottom of it; see the illustration.
This tape is going to be your
"half-court" line. It separates
the bowl into two halves.

2. Go on another bacteria and fungi safari
with your Scotch tape. Remember, stick your
tape onto a <u>single thing only</u>. Don't stick it to the
dog dish, then the sink, then the door knob …
just stick it to one thing only. Then take it back
to your agar dish. Lay the tape across the gel
from one side to the other. Pick it back up.

　　　Now you have two "teams." The tape stuck
to the outside bottom of your bowl is only there
so you can keep them separate.

3. Then, with a Q-tip (which should be sterile,
just out of the box), smear a little antibiotic from
your medicine cabinet onto one of your teams.
("Antibiotic" is a type of medicine designed to
kill bacteria. Neosporin and Bacitracin, for
example, are both common antibiotics.)

4. Once again, put your dish on a cool shelf
somewhere, out of the sun. Wait for results.
A week or two should do it.

Experiment Number
Tongue Life Comparisons

You'll need a shallow dish filled with a half-cup of agar gel.

1. Finally, your chance to prove who's got the cleanest mouth around. You'll need a new agar dish with a piece of tape stuck to the outside bottom as a half-court line.

2. Get your dog (or your sister, or brother, or whatever) to slobber on a sterile Q-tip.

3. Now, take <u>another</u> Q-tip and rub it around on <u>your</u> tongue.

4. Go back to your agar bowl and smear your opponent's Q-tip on one side, and <u>your</u> Q-tip on the other.

What Should Happen After a Week or Two in All Your Dishes

Things will start to grow on your agar. Those fuzzy little spots are actually little cities: millions upon millions of tiny life forms. Bacteria and fungi. They are eating your agar and loving it. There are probably more bacteria in any one of your dishes than there are people in New York.

Aureobasidium; decomposes paint

When you look in on your bacteria, <u>keep the plastic wrap on tight, don't take it off.</u>

Actinomycete, common soil-borne bacteria

Penicillium

Experiment Number 1 Results

Check this dish to see what your hunting luck was like. The more fuzzy spots you have on your gel—the more bacteria or fungi you picked up.

Penicillium with bacteria ringing it

Aureobasidium

Experiment Number 2 Results

In this second experiment, where you used antibiotic, you should see a clean, bacteria-free area where you smeared the medicine. If you don't, maybe you should consider switching brands.

Experiment Number 3 Results

What can I say? Whose tongue had the bigger, uglier bugs?

P.S. When you're done with your dishes, wash them out thoroughly.

Cladosporium, common airborne fungus

Aureobasidium

Yellow bacteria

White bacteria

HUMAN SPIT

Alternaria, common decay fungus

Bacteria

DOG LICK

Phoma

Aerobic soil bacterium
Pseudomonas fluorescens,
with whip-like tails

What's a Bacterium?

Life at its most basic. Bacteria are
among the oldest, simplest, and most
common forms of life on the planet. Currently,
scientists can separately identify some 2,500
different kinds of bacteria, but there are un-
questionably thousands more. Size-wise,
individual bacteria are not big players. The
period at the end of this sentence, for example,
would be the size of a city block to a lonely
bacterium sitting
in the middle of it.  BACTERIOPOLIS

Generally speaking, however, bacteria don't
often get off by themselves too much. They are
social creatures, living in large groups, and what
they lack in individual size they make up for in
an awesome birth rate.

40

What do I mean by "an awesome birth rate"?

Let's go back to that lonely bacterium that I mentioned a moment ago. The one that was sitting in the middle of that period. Let's pretend we could take it aside and adopt it—really treat it right. Give it all the food it could possibly eat, all the space it could possibly need. Keep all the bacteria-killers away. In short, let's imagine we could put it in bacterial paradise.

What would happen? In about three days, our single bacterium would have given birth to an extended bacterial family that would take up more space than the planet Earth.

Bacterial Heroes

For a beginning bacteriologist like yourself, probably the most surprising discovery you'll make is how unfairly bacteria have been treated over the years. Most people don't think about bacteria very much, but when they do, their thoughts are generally about things like infections, spoiled fruit, smelly socks, etc. As a result, most people don't have very positive feelings about bacteria or fungi.

But consider the following information for a little balance.

1 For more than two billion years, bacteria were the only life form on the planet. At the start of that time, neither the atmosphere nor the soil of planet Earth were capable of supporting complex life forms. At the end of that period, and largely thanks to the bacteria, the biosphere of the planet was ready to play host to the mind-boggling diversity of life that eventually led to you.

Complex Life Forms

2. Millions upon millions of individual bacteria call your body home. Nearly all of them are harmless stowaways, living their little lives on the surface of your skin, or in the air-exposed parts of your innards.

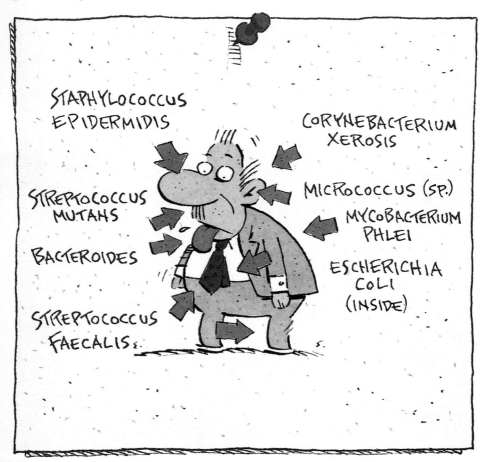

STAPHYLOCOCCUS
EPIDERMIDIS

CORYNEBACTERIUM
XEROSIS

STREPTOCOCCUS
MUTANS

MICROCOCCUS (SP.)

MYCOBACTERIUM
PHLEI

BACTEROIDES

ESCHERICHIA
COLI
(INSIDE)

STREPTOCOCCUS
FAECALIS

A small fraction are capable of doing you harm, if they get into the wrong places. But another fraction, probably a much larger fraction, are critical to your life. These are the bacteria that help break down your food in your intestines. If you could somehow rid your body of every bacterium in it, you would probably starve to death, regardless of how full your refrigerator was, because you could not digest your food.

3 This final point might be the most moving. Bacteria can and do get colds. In fact, when a bacterium gets a cold, or viral infection, he (she?) generally doesn't survive the experience. On the other hand, if they could somehow avoid any of the millions of hazards that are fatal for them, individual bacteria would not die of old age.

1

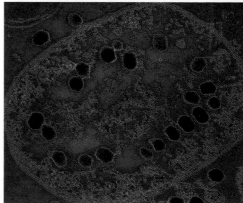

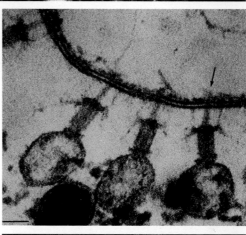

A stunning series of photographs, taken at increasing magnification, showing the actual moment of viral infection. The large oval shape is a bacterium under attack by a swarm of moon-lander-looking viruses. Since the viruses have no means of their own for self-replication, they inject their single strand of DNA (picture #2) into the victim bacterium in order to take over its reproductive machinery. In about 20 minutes, the takeover is complete (picture #3). The bacterium is filled with newly synthesized viruses (the black dots) and soon the walls of the bacterium will burst, spewing forth the viruses to start the process anew.

2

3

The Fungus Among Us

Bacteria are not the only life forms you'll be growing in your agar dish. Probably just as evident, perhaps even more so, will be cities of fungi, the fuzzy splotches you'll see on the agar gel.

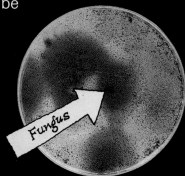

Bacteria and fungi are different. Fungi are bigger and haven't been around for as long as bacteria. (Fungi have been on Earth for about 400 million years. Bacteria, five times that.) They both have one thing in common, though. There are a lot of them. A wheelbarrowful of soil, for example, contains more fungi than there are people on the Earth.

On agar gel, *Alternaria* and *Aspergillus*, a spoilage fungus that can make toxins as a product of decay. Below, *Aspergillus Niger*, up close and personal.

45

As you might expect, fungi live very different lives from you or me, despite the fact that we share ancient ancestors. Fungi have no teeth, for one instance, and as a result they have to digest their food <u>before</u> they eat it. This is a dietary peculiarity which you may have stumbled upon. Perhaps you've bitten into an apple at some time, innocently expecting crisp goodness, only to spit out brown yuckiness?

From a scientific point of view, what you've actually done is interrupted a partially digested fungal meal. Left to themselves, the fungi will continue to soften the apple into a liquid and finally suck it up.

Despite our differences in eating habits, we do share one thing in common with fungi: We both use some of the same medicines.

Bacteria prey on fungi; they "eat" them, just as some of them prey on us. And since fungi have been dealing with the bacterial invasion problem for many more years than we have, they have developed some incredibly powerful chemical defenses —a few of which we have shamelessly stolen.

One particular kind of fungus, for example, secretes a chemical that is phenomenally poisonous to bacteria. In 1928, an English researcher by the name of Alexander Fleming was growing a dish of bacteria in a laboratory in London when he noticed that it had been contaminated by a rogue bit of fungus. His experiment ruined, he was in the process of throwing it all away when he noticed that the fungus had somehow managed to kill off all the bacteria around it. This was interesting enough to save for a little further investigation. Was the fungus giving off some kind of liquid "bacteria killer"?

Sir Alexander Fleming

It was. A clear, chemical substance. Since the fungus came from the penicillium family, Fleming named the liquid "penicillin" and it has probably been responsible for saving more human lives than any other single drug in the history of medicine. And although Alexander Fleming discovered it, "penicillin" was actually "invented" millions of years ago, by an anonymous, mutant fungus.

A dish of bacteria colonies contaminated by a penicillium fungus. The big circle is the area that's been clear-cut by the penicillin oozing out of the fungus seen in its middle.

In the ensuing years, many other antibiotics have been discovered in much the same
way—as naturally occurring fungal and bacterial products. (Streptomycin, aureomycin, and
erythromycin, for starters.) But most researchers believe that we are a long way from the bottom of this particular pile. Given that the vast
majority of bacterial and fungal types are as yet
undiscovered, the chances seem at least reason-
able that the cures to other ailments have long
since been created, and are now patiently waiting for a new discoverer. Perhaps one who is
not even a grown-up yet.

Perhaps a girl.
Perhaps a boy.
Perhaps you.

Light Wave Craziness

The streets of Hong Kong at night, as seen through a scratchy piece of glass that scatters light exactly like the scratchy piece of plastic right here in the book. The technical term for these scratchy filters, incidentally, is "diffraction gratings" and how you can play with them, as well as how they work, is what this section is all about.

Light Wave Craziness

What Is This Plastic Sheet?

There are several different answers to this question.

 A scratchy piece of plastic that shows pretty colors when you look at lights through it.

 A precisely manufactured plastic washboard whose scratches, or ridges, are so fine that they affect the direction of light waves that pass through them.

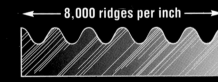

←——— 8,000 ridges per inch ———→

 A peephole into the very, very, very weird behavior of things that are very, very, very small.

WEIRD STUFF

How Can I Play With It?

 Easy. Hold it up to any source of indoor light. Look through it and you'll see a brilliant scatter of color radiating out from the bulb.

Different bulbs create different color patterns, so try looking at fluorescent bulbs (the tubular kind) as well as the normal, bulb-shaped, incandescent type.

 While you're at it, turn on the stove and look at the flame (or, if you're all-electric, at the glowing coils).

 If it's nighttime, try looking at street lamps, stop lights, the moon, and the very brightest stars. If a neon sign is around, it will make for a spectacular color scatter.

It's Very Pretty, But So What?

Take another look through the plastic. What I have been calling a "color scatter" is known in scientific circles as a color spectrum, and it is a "fingerprint" unique to whatever the light source is.

Since we're talking about "fingerprints," let's do a little detective work around the house.

If your stove is electric, look at the glowing coil. Now look at a normal, bulb-shaped, incandescent light. Which of the two has more blue? When you check for more blue, you're actually checking for higher temperature.

Compact discs are manufactured by digging rows upon rows of tiny little pits in the disc's surface. The rows are so close together that they diffract the incoming white light exactly as your plastic diffraction sheet does.

A good spectral detective can often tell you not only how hot something glowing is, but also exactly what it's made of.

For example: Let's say, through absolutely no fault of your own, you've become a murder suspect. The police come to your door to ask a few questions. You seem suspicious, so they examine your clothing. They find a tiny piece of something in your pant cuff. They take it back to the lab.

AHA?

They heat it to glowing, and look at the light it gives off through a piece of plastic like the one you have here. Then they take a picture of its unique color scatter or spectrum. (Okay, they actually look at it through a machine called a spectrometer, but it uses the same principle as your plastic.)

Then, they scrape a piece of paint off the victim's car and give it the same treatment, taking another picture.

Do the two pictures match? Tune in next week.

But police scientists aren't the most impressive spectral detectives by a long shot. That title belongs to the astronomers. With the help of a telescope, astronomers can look at the color scatter given off by a single star and tell you what it's made of, how hot it is, how fast it's moving, whether it's spinning, and whether anything is partially blocking its light. They can tell you all this, incidentally, about stars that are traveling near the speed of light at the edge of the visible universe, and that have been very, very dead since long before the Earth was born.

No matter how you slice it, that's impressive detective work.

EUREKA!

Are Stars Star-shaped?

Nope. The reason artists of all ages have drawn stars that way for millenia is because they have bad eyes. So do you, for that matter.

The surface of your eye is called the cornea, and, as the years wear on, it becomes scratched, just like a diffraction grating. A scratched cornea is not a very good diffraction grating, but it will work if you look at a star, a point source of light against a dark background. Then, instead of seeing a point, you'll see a spiky shape. And, if there are some temperature differences in the atmosphere that night (there usually are), the spiky shape will shimmer and twinkle.

Scratched corneas, incidentally, are a particular problem in Middle Eastern countries where the wind and sand combine to do a great deal of eye damage.

What's Going On?

When you hold up this scratchy plastic to a light bulb, you are peering into one of the quirkiest, most fundamentally odd parts of our universe—light. Some of the very best scientific minds of the past three centuries have devoted their careers to the study of light and its ultimate nature. Don't be alarmed though. This explanation is written by and for normal human beings.

Light can behave like a wave. More than 300 years' worth of scientists will back me up on this. Go to the beach, sit and stare at the waves rolling in and you'll get a pretty good idea of waveness. Keep that idea in mind for a second and imagine waves of light, rolling out from a light bulb. Some of them are born short waves, and they are bluish; some are born long, and they're reddish. They jumble together and look white to our eyes. At least until you un-jumble them with your plastic sheet. Here's how it works.

Go back to the beach. Build a picket fence a little way out. Notice that a wave hitting the backside of the fence turns into a lot of little waves as it funnels through the pickets. Plus, the pickets change the waves' direction. The longer the wave, the more it bends coming through.

Physicists measure wavelength from peak to peak.

Surfers measure wave height top to bottom.

55

Now here comes a jump, so hang on. Go from your picket fence in the surf to your scratchy piece of plastic in the path of a light wave. The scratches work the same as your fence pickets. As the light waves hit the back of the plastic sheet, they are bent by the scratches. Longer waves (red light) bend more than shorter waves (blue). Result? White light gets sorted out into its colors (■ + ■ + ■ = ☐).

On one level, that's a complete explanation. You can stop right here if you want to and you should do fine on the quiz. However, I do want to talk about something else, and you can come along if you're attracted by things a little strange. It has to do with another facet of light.

Extra Credit

Light, it turns out, is a very peculiar animal— the platypus of the micro-world. It is far easier to talk about how it behaves than what exactly it is.

A few paragraphs ago I said that light behaved like a wave. That's true. It's also true that sometimes it behaves like tiny balls, or particles ("photons," the scientists say). Sometimes we see light doing things and we can best describe them in terms of waveness. Other times we see light doing things and we can best describe them in terms of particleness.

For years scientists went around and around on this single point: Is light a wave, vibrating out from its source? Or is it a stream of tiny particles, shooting out from a light bulb?

It's a puzzle. We can explain the colors you see coming through your diffraction grating very satisfactorily in terms of waves getting "squeezed" through a "picket fence."

But here's the weird thing. When scientists set up equipment behind a "picket fence" in order to detect the waves as they come through, it turns out that the light arrives in particles. The conclusion? Light is extremely curious. Scientists currently believe it is both wave and particle (a warticle?)

Let me conclude before you run off. What you've stuck your nose into here, just by looking through your piece of plastic, is an area of physics called "quantum mechanics." Don't be frightened. I'm not going to go into it in any detail, but I do want to say this: It's very, very interesting, it's only about 50 years old, it's stood up to every experiment ever devised to disprove it, and it plays a practical role in every electronic device manufactured today. Oh yes, and Einstein had some problems with it.

Richard Feynman, a Nobel prize-winning physicist who wrote and taught about quantum mechanics for many years, once said the entire field was contained in a single, very puzzling experiment called the "double-slit" experiment. He went on to say that nobody really, truly understood the double-slit experiment. I'll only add one comment to that: The double-slit experiment he was referring to is a very finely controlled version of looking through a diffraction grating, something you just did.

57

Diffracted Lightning Bolt

As a bolt of lightning streaks through the atmosphere, it generates unearthly air temperatures (they exceed the surface temperature of the sun, for example). Billions of nearby gas molecules and atoms are excited ("charged up") by this extreme energy. An instant later, they "discharge" their energy in the form of light.

Each discharging gas molecule or atom emits a particular color of light, depending on which type of gas it is (oxygen and nitrogen are the two most common, yielding red and blue). To our eyes, the discharged light is a mix (white), but the diffraction grating "unmixes" the white into its constituent colors.

Incidentally, lightning storms occur somewhere on the planet at the rate of about 40,000 per day, generating more than 100 lightning flashes per second. This particular bolt was photographed from the roof of the physics building at the University of Arizona by Professor William Bickel.

Homemade Science

Homemade Science

If you're at home right now reading this, looking at that headline and worrying about doing any science at home because you don't have a Nobel prize-winning laboratory, you can relax. Your house is a better laboratory than most historical scientists ever had. There are probably more chemicals, tools, measuring devices, and experimental equipment in your kitchen than existed in any scientific laboratory up until about 200 years ago.

In this section, we're going to prove it. We're going to use what is probably the most spectacular piece of experimental equipment we hope you already own. It's a recent invention. It's probably in your bathroom. A scientist might call it a "laminar flow gas propulsion device." We'll call it your hair dryer.

A Word About Hair Dryer Safety

Talk to your grown-up assistant about using a hair dryer. They are not toys and you have to be careful with them.

The Prime Rule is this: Never, never, never use a hair dryer near any water, like a full sink or bathtub.

Hair dryers are electric, and water conducts electricity. The combination is potentially deadly.

Also, hair dryers get **HOT**

Be careful with them.

If you block the flow of your hair dryer, or if you leave it on too long and it overheats, it should shut off automatically. Let it cool off for a few minutes before you start it again.

Don't block the flow.

Last but not least. If you have a vacuum cleaner with a hose that you can stick in one end or the other, you're in luck. Plug the hose into the exhaust end of your vacuum cleaner and you won't even need a hair dryer.

Turn the heat down if you can.

Don't touch the end of your hair dryer when it gets hot. If yours has a heat control separate from the strength control, turn it to its lowest heat.

AIR   low
HEAT
low
high

How Do I Use It?
Balloon Research

Go find a round balloon and blow it up. Turn on your hair dryer and point the air flow straight up. Place the balloon in the rushing air. Experiment with the various strength settings (max is probably the best). Fool around until you can get the balloon to stay put without any touching. (A ping-pong ball, incidentally, will also work.)

Just for fun, see how far you can tip the hair dryer down until the balloon falls to the ground.

Next, point the dryer straight up again and whip your open hand through the column of air. Do it slower and slower until it disrupts the air enough to make the balloon fall out. Then, turn the dryer off with the balloon mid-air. As the balloon falls, catch it as it comes down using only the end of your dryer. Then turn it back on and see if you can get the balloon hovering again. All with no hands, of course.

Finally, move over to a wall for the biggest effect. Hold the dryer right next to the wall, point it straight up and put the balloon back in the air. It should hover about a foot or so higher (the wall works as a maximizer). A corner works even better.

For a possible team activity,
toss the balloon up in the air and
"catch" it on the rushing air.
If you have a co-researcher
who is similarly equipped,
it is possible to play a
no-hands game of balloon catch.
(Extension cords are helpful).

Heavy Scientific Breathing

For this part, you can put away your hair dryer. You won't be needing it anymore. What you <u>will</u> be needing is a big spool of thread, a thumbtack, and a 3x5 card,
or a playing card.
Go get them.
This is worth it.

You're back. Stick the thumbtack into the middle of the card. Then make sure the hole through your spool is clear. Blow through it to check. Now, take a deep breath, point your spool toward the ground and blow through it. Steady and medium hard. At the same time, gently press your card to the other end of the spool. Stick the point of the thumbtack into the hole. If you're blowing firmly and steadily, and if the card is dead flat, you can pull your hand away. The card will not blow away. It will stick to the spool.

Here's another exercise in anti-gravity research.

You'll need a big kitchen funnel and a balloon, or, even better, a ping-pong ball. The procedure is very much the same as before. Put the small end of the funnel to your mouth and blow steadily and firmly straight down, toward the ground. Now, before you run out of wind, stick the balloon (or ping-pong ball) into the wide end of the funnel. Remove hand. Presto! The Amazing Anti-Gravity Wind Funnel!

Hair Dryer Science

Why does a balloon or ping-pong ball hover inside a column of rushing air?

Basically, the answer is simple. (Well, half of it is, anyway.)

If something bounces off of something else, that something else gets pushed away by the impact. It's what happens when you hit a milk carton with a baseball. The carton gets knocked over. Big surprise.

The same thing happens when you stick your open hand outside a car window and hold it flat, edge-on to the wind. You won't feel any "lift." But if you turn it at an angle, the wind will hit your palm, bounce off it, and force your hand up.

A balloon over your hair dryer is getting hit by a lot of air, but since the air bounces <u>out</u>, the balloon gets pushed <u>in</u>. "In" means the balloon gets pushed into the center of the column of air where it gets lifted until gravity stops it from going any higher.

That's half the answer. Here's the other part.

As the balloon sits in the stream of air, a low-pressure area is directly over it. It's there simply because the wind is being blocked. Imagine a crowd pouring through a big room. A pillar in the middle of the room is blocking its path and the crowd splits around it. Directly behind the pillar there are not many people: It's a "people low-pressure" area.

Of course the empty space is not very big because the people start ducking into it as they rush by, filling it back up. Think of those people as they rush into the uncrowded space as a sideways "jet" of people.

The same thing happens to the empty space on the backside of the balloon. As the air rushing by turns to fill up the space, that air also becomes a sideways "jet." It fills in the empty space, and then tries to keep right on going—out the side of the main column. (People wouldn't keep right on going, but the air does.)

As the sideways jet rushes "out" it pushes "back" on the balloon. What ends up happening is this: The outgoing jet pushes the balloon back into the column of air every time the balloon begins to wander out.

These two competing jets "kick" the balloon from both sides to keep it dead center.

You can feel this "sideways air" yourself very easily. Simply hold the balloon <u>halfway</u> in the main jet of air. Keep hanging on to it; then, with your other hand, feel around for the jet coming off the top. This force you feel pulling on the balloon is <u>precisely</u> the same force that keeps an airplane up. (The next time you look out a window at 30,000 feet you might think about this for a moment. You may have many reasons for traveling, but that little tug on the balloon is the only reason you have for staying up in the air.)

Since the air goes
this way ...

...the balloon is kicked
back this way.

But What About the Spool and the Anti-Gravity Card?

The principle at work here is different. Imagine that you felt destructive for a moment and drilled a small hole in your car's windshield. Later, whizzing down the highway, you pushed a paper plate up against the hole to stop the wind from coming through. Wouldn't the plate get blown away by the air?

The answer is "no." It would stick to the windshield just like the card stuck to the spool. For the reasons, you'll have to meet Daniel Bernoulli, the Swiss scientist who discovered the operating principle 200 years ago.

Daniel Bernoulli (1700–1782)

Here is how it is generally stated: "A flowing fluid, or gas, will lower the barometric pressure of the area it occupies. The faster it flows, the lower the pressure."

Translation: If you shoot a fluid (water from a garden hose, air from a hair dryer) the stream will suck any "bystanders" into it. The "bystanders" are usually surrounding gases, and they are sucked in because things that are fluid (water, people who are walking, gases, etc.) move away from areas of high pressure and towards areas of low pressure.

If the word "pressure" is confusing you, use the word "crowded"; it means nearly the same thing. (A crowded room is a room of "high people pressure.")

Here's more proof that Bernoulli had it right. Roll your window down a crack the next time you're in a car. Hold a strip of paper near the opening. It doesn't just hang there, of course, nor is it blown <u>toward</u> you, as you might have guessed. Just like Dan Bernoulli predicted, it is sucked <u>out</u> the window by the lower pressure that exists in the stream of air outside your car.

Now. Let's talk specifically about the little card on the spool (or the paper plate on the windshield, or the balloon in the funnel—they all work the same way). Here is what happens:

When a rush of air (like your breath) hits something (like a little card, or a balloon) all the air gets shot off to the side. Result? Sideways moving air. Enter Mr. Bernoulli. Moving air means bystanders are going to get sucked in. But in these special cases, the only "bystanders" are paper plates, cards, balloons, or ping-pong balls. The air rushes by them, they get sucked in, so when you move your hand away, there they stick. Amazing.

Nature's Own Hair Dryer

As you will remember, Dorothy's trip to Oz was made possible by a Kansas tornado that lifted her house clear of its foundations and then, some time later, dropped it onto the unpleasant lady with the nice shoes.

You may have wondered about the science behind this voyage. Actually, it's not that bad. Tornado winds have never been accurately clocked, but 200–300 miles an hour is a conservative estimate. When put into a wind of that speed, things that don't look very much like wings can suddenly start acting like them; roofs, for example.

Roofless houses are a common sight in the track of a tornado and the reason is quite aerodynamic: The roofs didn't blow off so much as fly off. The wind pours over the roof and down the backside of the building. This is precisely the effect you felt when you held your balloon only partway into the windstream. The tug you felt was the same as a roof might feel when a tornado hits it. In essence, the wind goes one way, the roof goes the other.

Getting back to Dorothy, we can only assume that her roof was fastened to the walls with particular care. As a result, when her roof started to fly away, unlike most of them, it took the house along with it.

Activity:
Flying Quarters

You can fly a quarter off the top of a table using some of these very same Dorothy-tested principles. Simply lay a quarter on a table a few inches from the edge. Squat down and blow very hard directly over the quarter. The front edge of the quarter will be lifted by the low pressure in the airflow over it, and then it will be caught by the full force of the wind and flip.

What's Wrong with this Picture?

We took this photograph and flopped the negative before we printed it. So everything left of center went right, and everything right of center went left. It's the same as looking into a mirror. Your job is to un-flop the photo by looking at it through the mirror here. Then try to find the 14 things that are wrong with it. Hint: Keep in mind where his left and right are.

Bouncing Light Rays

What Is It?

An efficient, highly organized light ray bouncer. Man-made organized light ray bouncers have been in use for at least 7,000 years, the first ones probably being made of polished obsidian, a naturally occurring glassy material. The kind you looked at this morning, over the sink, is a clear piece of glass with a silver coating on the back. The ancient Greeks made mirrors the same way, over 2,000 years ago.

Mirror Maze

A well-known researcher, G.M. Stratton, once conducted an experiment on himself that has become a psychology classic. For eight continuous days, he wore a homemade pair of glasses that flipped everything upside-down. What surprised him the most, he later wrote, was his brain's eventual ability to make the necessary adjustments. By the seventh day, he was getting around quite well; "upside-down" was becoming normal.

This maze is a quick version of the same idea. It should give you an idea of what Dr. Stratton's first few upside-down days must have felt like, *before* his brain adjusted.

Instructions: Lay the book flat, then prop up the mirror page so you can see the maze in it. Now, in order to keep you from looking at the maze directly, put a stack of books in front of it. Then, looking *only* through the mirror, try to trace the eraser end of a pencil through the maze. No fair looking directly at your hand or the maze.

75

How Can I
Play With It?

Stare at the
mirror for a
moment. Try
to be objective.
What do you
see? A vision
of breathtak-
ing beauty?
The pinnacle
of human evolution?

That's right, you star, it's you. At least, it's
you the way you think you look. The world, of
course, knows a different you. They see a face
whose right and left sides haven't been swapped
in a mirror. If you want to see that face, the one
everyone else has to deal with, you'll need to
bend the mirror a little bit.
Stand the book up and look
into the mirror while you
make a trough out of it.
Do it slowly. At first you'll
see nothing but scrambled
colors, but at a certain point,
your face will come into focus. Make
some fine bending adjustments until it
looks just right. There. That's you with your
right and left sides in place, the way everybody
else sees you. Still pretty impressive,
though, huh?

Now wink at yourself. It'll look strange—backwards somehow. Flatten the mirror and wink again. That should look normal. It's not, of course. A lifetime of staring at mirrors has inverted your self-image. What's <u>really</u> normal is in the bent mirror, that's the face you put to the world. The other one, the face in the flat mirror, is the flopped one. You're about the only person who ever has to see that face.

THE FRANK QUIZ: Frank's unfortunate scar is over his left eye. Knowing that, which of these faces do you think Frank looks at every morning as he prepares to lather up and shave?

Activity:
So You Think You Can Count Your Fingers?

Open your book to the mirror and prop it up in front of another mirror, so that the two mirrors are facing one another about a foot apart. Put your hand in between the two of them and spread your fingers. Look into the mirror and move your head around until you can see as many images of your hand as you possibly can. Then start counting fingers. Theoretically, a total of about 80 should be possible. Here at the Exploratorium, using glass mirrors, our best finger-counter can do 45.

The T-Shirt in the Mirror Question

Q. How come when I look in the mirror, and I'm wearing my T-shirt, my T-shirt looks weird—**"ꟽYƆ Ꙅ'ꓷ⅃Oꓯ"**—but I still look like a million bucks?

A. Symmetry. You can look it up. It means the right side of something looks like the left side. Your face, for example, is symmetric. Unless your left eye is five times bigger than your right, you look about the same in a mirror (when your image is flopped) as you do in a photograph (when it's not).

However, the writing on your shirt is <u>not</u> symmetric. **"GOLD'S GYM"** does not look the same as **"ꟽYƆ Ꙅ'ꓷ⅃Oꓯ"**.

Activity:
Writing Upside Down and Back Words

While it is certainly true that the vast majority of the words in the English language are not symmetric, there are a few notable exceptions. What follows is a list of them. They will read the same if they are held <u>upside down</u> in a mirror. Try it. Your task is to write a very, very short story, using only these words. (For example:

HICKOK DIED DEC 3 1883—
DOC BEECH DECIDED HE CHOKED)

If your story is a good bit more interesting than ours, send it to **The Klutz Press Back Words Contest;** we'll read it in a mirror, and we'll find some suitable prizes to send the winners.

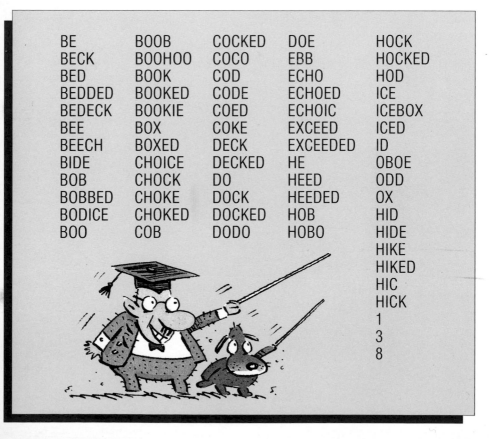

BE	BOOB	COCKED	DOE	HOCK
BECK	BOOHOO	COCO	EBB	HOCKED
BED	BOOK	COD	ECHO	HOD
BEDDED	BOOKED	CODE	ECHOED	ICE
BEDECK	BOOKIE	COED	ECHOIC	ICEBOX
BEE	BOX	COKE	EXCEED	ICED
BEECH	BOXED	DECK	EXCEEDED	ID
BIDE	CHOICE	DECKED	HE	OBOE
BOB	CHOCK	DO	HEED	ODD
BOBBED	CHOKE	DOCK	HEEDED	OX
BODICE	CHOKED	DOCKED	HOB	HID
BOO	COB	DODO	HOBO	HIDE
				HIKE
				HIKED
				HIC
				HICK
				1
				3
				8

Q. How come everyone mixes up their left and right, and no one mixes up their up and down?

A. Although this is not strictly a mirror question, I'm glad you asked me this, because it's something that I have often wondered about myself. I have a couple of theories.

One: The Gravity Theory. Down = "the way gravity goes" and gravity is a powerful reminder. (Example: You're on a cliff. Do you wonder which direction you'll go if you step off?) If we lived in a weightless environment, "down" would be "feet direction" and "up" would be "head direction." I suspect there would be a good bit more confusion under those circumstances.

Two: The Feet vs. Head Theory. While your left hand looks more or less like your right hand, your head does not look more or less like your feet—hopefully. Since our eyes are in our heads, we have a built-in upside reminder. If our eyes were in our stomachs, and if we had another pair of feet on our shoulders, then we'd be symmetric in the up and down direction as well as the left and right direction. As a result, up-and-downness would be subject to the same look-alike confusion as left-and-rightness. Right?

Barbershop Lasers

The next time you get your hair cut, and find yourself staring at all those images of yourself that go marching off into infinity, you might mention to the barber that both of you are actually standing directly in the guts of a low-tech laser.

Sort of.

A regular laser consists (in essence) of a light source stuck in between two precisely parallel mirrors. If you were to bring a flashlight with you the next time you went to the barber, you could get a better idea of the process by pointing it at one of the mirrors and turning it on.

If you could somehow keep your flashlight from getting in the way of the bounced-back beam, the light would go back and forth a few dozen times before it faded out. The reason it fades, incidentally, is that barbershop mirrors aren't that reflective; they eat up about 10% of the light that hits them. In addition, they aren't exactly parallel.

Real lasers have much better mirrors that are aligned to within one 10-millionth of an inch. Plus, the light source is ordinarily not a flashlight. Instead they use a glowing gas (some gases will glow if an electric charge is put to them—neon, for example).

In order to contain the gas and hold the mirrors, lasers are normally built in a tube shape.

As the light passes through the glowing gas on its way back and forth between mirrors, a strange thing happens. Instead of dying away, it actually becomes strengthened. On every pass it strikes billions of atoms of the gas, "stimulating" them. And when they become stimulated, they give off more light of the same color as the incoming light. That light, in turn, bounces off the mirrors and stimulates more atoms to give off more light, which then stimulates more atoms to give off more light, which then stimulates more atoms to give off more light . . .

By timing the return trip of a bounced laser beam, it is possible to determine —within inches—the location of objects such as the moon and man-made satellites.

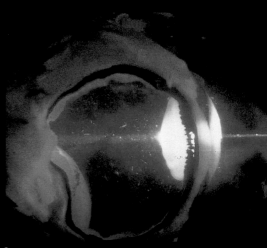

1

Obviously there's a limit to this process, but it is still an enormously powerful feedback effect. Without it, lasers would not be possible.

Some pulse type of lasers let the light bounce back and forth between the mirrors for quite a few round trips (as many as 100) before a mechanism allows the light to escape. It's as if one of the mirrors was suddenly moved aside to reveal a doorway. When the pulse escapes, it can carry a tremendous amount of energy. Eye doctors, for example, use these types of lasers to do extremely precise kinds of surgery. In some cases, an eye surgeon will direct a laser beam through the clear lens of the eye—without damaging it—before the beam strikes the opaque retina, where it will cut far more sharply than any scalpel.

2

The laser as healer. An ophthalmologist carefully directs a beam through the clear lens of the patient's eye onto the retina in the back of the eye (picture #2) where it can "weld" a detached retina back into place.

Moiré Spinner

The little spinner on the cover of this book is called a moiré (mwar-ay) spinner. Printed on the plastic piece is a repeating pattern of circles. Directly underneath it, the same pattern is printed on the cover. When you spin the plastic piece, the two patterns line up, and then misalign. Although the pattern is definitely "real," it exists only in your eye, where the two images are "added up."

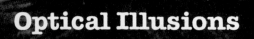

Optical Illusions

Illusions

Is this a perfect square?

Who Are You Going to Believe? Me? Or Your Own Eyes?

Me. And I'll show you why.

Take the three fellows in the photo you see to the right here. Look particularly at the image of the chap on the right, with the height problem. Your task is to rank the three images of the men in size— biggest, smallest, and in-between.

While you're thinking about that, look at the photo of these two young ladies below. Take a good look. Now rank them for height.

Finally, look back at the divider page. Regard the upside-down Elvis. Then turn him over.

Who's taller?

Who's tallest?
Who's shortest?

What's Going On Here?

From your brain's point of view, life is a staggering blast of completely disorganized stuff. Impressions, feelings, images, smells, etc., are being fire-hosed into your brain through your eyes, ears, nose, and skin every waking hour. It's confusing, never-ending, and hopelessly chaotic.

At least it would be, if your brain didn't create an internal filing system to organize it. This filing system is mostly unconscious, and the process of how it works is multi-layered and very complex, but the biggest, most important step is probably the first: Most of what goes into your brain, it simply throws away. (There are millions of examples. One would be the sensation your shoes make against your feet. Your brain generally ignores it.)

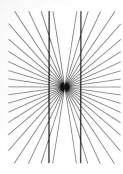

Are the two blue lines straight?

If your brain did not "edit" the input like this, or organize the rest into familiar patterns, you would undoubtedly be paralyzed by the onslaught. In fact, psychologists believe that some forms of mental illness stem from faulty organizational "wiring." The patient experiences "too much" and as a result, fails to put it into patterns.

Fraser's Spiral

Perhaps the most enduring of all the printed optical illusions, Fraser's spiral refuses to "correct" itself even after you understand the illusion. Much as your brain wants to deny it, the "spiral" is not a spiral, but in fact concentric circles, as the inset shows.

This basic fact of life often comes as a surprise, especially to those of us who are clearly not very organized. But there's plenty of proof. In fact, you've just gone through a proof. Illusions, optical as well as most of the other kind, demonstrate this unconscious organization process because they trip it up. They are the exceptions that prove the rule. An illusion sets up an "ordinary" scene, gives our brains all the regular cues, and then pulls out the chair at the last instant.

But note the most interesting part of all this. It's not the punch line, when your brain goes sprawling (as funny as that is). Instead, it's in the setup. That's the proof that your brain has trained itself to operate in a blindered, not very bright-seeming kind of way.

For example: Try this riddle, which I hope everyone hasn't heard already.

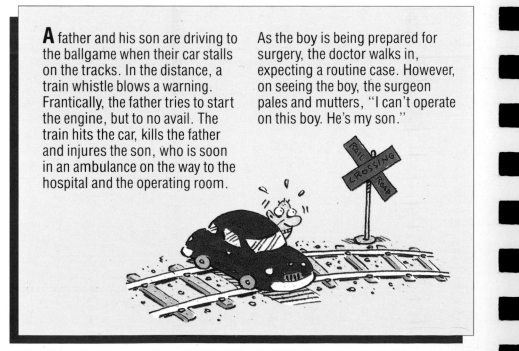

A father and his son are driving to the ballgame when their car stalls on the tracks. In the distance, a train whistle blows a warning. Frantically, the father tries to start the engine, but to no avail. The train hits the car, kills the father and injures the son, who is soon in an ambulance on the way to the hospital and the operating room.

As the boy is being prepared for surgery, the doctor walks in, expecting a routine case. However, on seeing the boy, the surgeon pales and mutters, "I can't operate on this boy. He's my son."

As you've probably suspected, the answer to this little puzzle is painfully obvious. It's right there in front of you. If you haven't got it, it just means that your brain is hop-skipping over it. You have to slow down and examine every assumption you're making, particularly the unconscious ones.

There is no triangle in this drawing. There are three circle-looking things with bites taken out of them.

For a photographic version of a similar process, look again at the photograph of the three men. All its life your brain has been dealing with distant things. It knows that people at the end of the block are not one inch tall, they just look that way. When it sees a person moving their legs and starting to enlarge, it's not fooled. It knows what's really happening. Somebody is walking toward it.

Since your brain invariably works this way, no matter what it's looking at, we decided we'd set it up for a harmless little practical joke. In the photo of the three men, your brain sees the small character in the background the same way it always sees small characters—as distant people—and <u>unconsciously it heightens the image to compensate for its distance</u>. No problem there. But then with the help of a pair of scissors, we put the same character in the foreground. Now what? Your brain sees a foreground image, so the "automatic heighten" button does not get pushed, and the result is the two images don't match up.

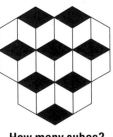

How many cubes?

Actually, though, they <u>do</u> match up, as you can demonstrate to your disbelieving brain with a ruler. (You might also mention to your brain that surgeons are not always men.)

Giovanni Paolo Panini's
Interior of Saint Peter's, Rome (1746/1754)

Perspective in the hands of a master artist. Even though it's impossible, the viewer can stare down the long hall of this two-dimensional piece of paper. In addition, if you holler at this painting, you can hear the echo.

This ability to create the illusion of three dimensions on a flat piece of canvas or paper was discovered in Europe in the early 1400s. Previous to that, perspective illusion technique was unknown. Just as children do today, medieval and classical artists painted foreground figures the same size as background figures, creating a flat, unreal look.

The Moon Illusion

Ever since a hairy <u>Homo sapiens</u> looked up from a cold dinner of pterodactyl drumstick and watched the full moon rise over a belching volcano, humankind has been puzzled by an apparent paradox: Why does the moon seem to shrink as it climbs in the sky?

We all know the effect: At moonrise, on the horizon, the full moon is enormous, while a few hours later, in the midst of a black sky, it has shrunk back to relative insignificance.

Everyone from that first mastodon-muncher on up to today's astrophysicists have proposed theories to explain it. (An entire book was recently published on the subject.) But the explanation that seems to enjoy the most popularity these days is the same one we just went through. You might call it the "Automatic Heighten Button Theory."

On the horizon, with buildings or trees in the foreground, the moon is perceived as a background object. As a result, the "Automatic Heighten" button gets unconsciously pushed and the moon becomes "enlarged." (Remember the doctored photo of the three men?)

Hours later, with no more foreground buildings or landscape to compare it with, the moon itself becomes the "foreground" and the button is <u>not</u> pushed. The result is an <u>apparent</u> difference in size. But, if you hold a dime at arm's length, when the next full moon comes up, you'll see the dime and the moon just about match up. A couple of hours later, do the same thing. Even though the moon looks a lot smaller, the "dime test" will give the same results.

A Few More Answers

Take another look at Rachel and Rebecca, our twins who don't look like twins. All its life, your brain has been living in square rooms. When it sees things in a room it says to itself, "Aha! Room. Must be square. They all are."

Of course, the room our twins are standing in isn't. As a result, all the assumptions your brain makes about height and perspective are wrong, and it comes to the wrong conclusions.

We used a related strategy in putting together the Elvis photo. As you look at the big picture on our Elvis page, your brain's overriding impression is simply an upside-down photo of The King. Seems relatively normal. But your brain is a raw beginner at looking at upside-down people—it doesn't see very many—so we took advantage of that. We made the eyes and mouth normal (i.e., we turned them right-side up) and put them back on. So, your brain takes a quick look at the photo and says, "upside-down head; eyes, mouth normal. Seems OK."

But turn the photo over, and all sorts of bells and sirens go off. Now the big picture is highly familiar (your brain knows what right-side-up people ought to look like) and something as weird as upside-down eyes and mouth scream at you.

Your Brain, the Shortcut Taker

Illusions, like the ones you've just looked at, take advantage of the fact that your brain generally knows how to fast-forward past the obvious stuff. It's also stored billions of pieces of unconscious data and uses them unthinkingly to make sense of the world. It has to. But the process can be carried to extremes.

If you fell for the surgeon riddle, as I did, you've seen an example of the problem. Most surgeons are men, so your brain takes a shortcut. It hears the world "surgeon" and says to itself "male." Say the word "nurse" and your brain barely wakes up enough to say "female."

The word for this kind of thing isn't just "mental shortcut," it's more like "bias" or "prejudice." Some people get such a bad case of it that they start saying things like "Surgeons <u>ought</u> to be men," or "Nurses <u>ought</u> to be women."

That kind of thinking can lead to real problems. But now that you know where it comes from, you can take some active steps to prevent it. Just give your brain a real wake-up call whenever you suspect it might be taking one of these lazy shortcuts that it shouldn't.

. . . .

Your Final Exam:
What's Wrong with this Caption?

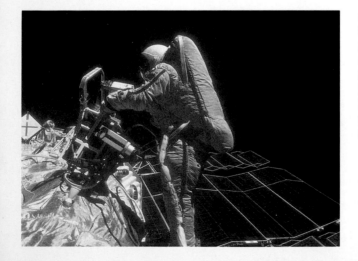

A Russian cosmonaut works with equipment designed for use in outer space. The spacesuit he's wearing is designed to protect him from the harsh conditions of the airless environment.

Now for the quiz: I'm lying somewhere in this caption. Where? Answer on last page.

About the Exploratorium

The Explorabook was created over a period of nearly three years of intensive collaboration between the editors of Klutz Press and the staff of the San Francisco Exploratorium.

The Exploratorium, a place of scientific imagination, was begun in 1969 by Dr. Frank Oppenheimer. Located in the shadow of the Golden Gate Bridge, it is housed in the historic Palace of Fine Arts, a cavern of a building constructed for the Pan-Pacific International Exposition of 1915.

The museum was founded on Dr. Oppenheimer's practical conviction that nothing is ever learned until it is self-taught, and that the preferred position for this kind of learning is vertical: both feet on the ground and both arms elbow-deep in the subject matter.

Officially, the Exploratorium describes itself as "a museum of science, art, and human perception," and its goal "to help visitors ask their own questions—about the world and their perception of it." Unofficially, the operating philosophy is that this whole process ought to be a kick in the pants.

There are over 600 exhibits at the Exploratorium. They're called "exhibits," but it's actually a poor choice of words. Nothing is inside a display case. Nothing is behind a velvet-covered chain. To just look at an Exploratorium exhibit is to miss the point of it, and it doesn't take long for most visitors to discover that.

The inside of the Exploratorium is a vast open space. In keeping with the freewheeling spirit of the place, there are few walls. On any given day, it is usually swarming with visitors (newly turned research scientists). They are laughing, talking, rushing from one invented exhibit to the next, stopping at each to pull, push, poke, probe, prod, shake, and, if necessary, crawl underneath in order to see what makes them all tick.

The result of all this activity is an atmosphere that is open, exciting and playful. The Exploratorium does not look like a museum. It looks like Santa's workshop, overrun by a tribe of techno-elves.

When we began the Explorabook, we said we wanted to take the Exploratorium (all 100,000 square feet of it) and squeeze it between covers. We tried mightily. If we caught just a fraction of the spirit of this very special institution, we'll consider this project a brave success.

We would like to make the last few words of this book an invitation. Actually, two invitations. One to visit the Exploratorium itself at 3601 Lyon Street, San Francisco (tel. 415-563-7337), and the other to explore the worlds that lie behind each of the subjects touched upon here in this book. These are worlds with zillions of wild and woolly continents, poorly charted and in desperate need of explorers. We very sincerely hope you decide to poke around on some of them.

Photo Credits

**Answer to the Final Exam on page 97:
The cosmonaut's name is Svetlana
Savitskaya, and she is a mother of three.**